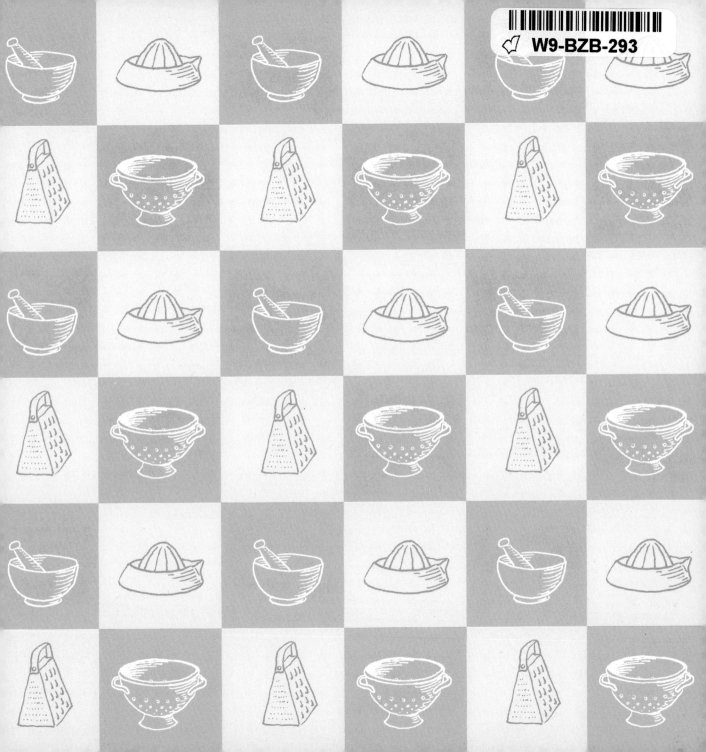

GINGER

GINGER

A Book of Recipes

INTRODUCTION BY PEPITA ARIS

LORENZ BOOKS
NEW YORK • LONDON • SYDNEY • BATH

First published by Lorenz Books in 1996

© 1996 Anness Publishing Limited

Lorenz Books is an imprint of
Anness Publishing Limited
Boundary Row Studios
1 Boundary Row
London SE1 8HP

This edition distributed in Canada by
Raincoast Books Distribution Limited

Distributed in Australia by Reed Books Australia

ISBN 1 85967 152 7

Publisher Joanna Lorenz
Senior Cookery Editor Linda Fraser
Cookery Editor Anne Hildyard
Designer Lilian Lindblom
Illustrations Anna Koska
Photographers Karl Adamson, Edward Allwright, Steve Baxter, James Duncan, Michelle Garrett,
Don Last and Michael Michaels
Recipes Alex Barker, Roz Denny, Nicola Diggins, Rafi Fernandez, Christine France, Sarah Gates,
Shirley Gill, Deh-Ta Hsiung, Sue Maggs, Liz Trigg and Steven Wheeler
Food for photography Carole Handslip, Wendy Lee and Jane Stevenson
Stylists Madeleine Brehaut, Hilary Guy, Maria Kelly, Blake Minton, Kirsty Rawlings and Fiona Tillett
Jacket photography Amanda Heywood

Typeset by MC Typeset Ltd, Rochester, Kent
Printed in Singapore by Star Standard Industries Pte. Ltd.

Contents

$\mathscr{I}$NTRODUCTION

Who has not stopped to savor the delicious smell of ginger cooking? Whether it's the comforting and homely aroma of gingerbread baking on a winter's day or an intriguing burst of oriental promise, ginger has immediate appeal at all meals, sweet and savory, all the year round.

Ginger has been a kitchen staple for more than a millennium – its use in Chinese cooking dates back to 200BC. Powdered ginger journeyed to Northern Europe early; it is the one Asiatic spice which predates introduction by the Crusaders. Its associations were, historically, wintry: bringing cheer at the coldest, dreariest time of year. Gingerbread is one of the oldest cake-breads in the world and is now found in every northern country, usually associated with Christmas and other winter festivals. Preserved ginger, in syrup, in handsome blue and white jars that are now prized in their own right, came to Europe early in the eighteenth century from China.

Of course, ginger is used in most of Asia, and its flavor is central to the characteristic spice blends of a wide variety of oriental cuisines. Scallions, ginger and garlic are the classic note of Chinese recipes; in India, the combination of ginger with onions and garlic is evident equally in North Indian sauces and in the vegetarian dishes that are the delight of southern states such as

Gujarat. Ground ginger is included in spice mixes and is popular in the rich dishes of Mogul cuisine – as it is, incidentally, in Moroccan cooking, one of the most refined of North Africa. And as Japanese and South-East Asian cooking becomes more common all over the world, the popularity of ginger has increased.

Ginger is sold as a fresh root, dried whole, ground to powder, preserved in syrup and crystallized. Each form has a subtly different flavor, but common to all is a sweet and pungent spiciness.

The recipes in the book use all the forms to their best advantage and draw inspiration from all over the world. They begin with simple yet exotic soups and first courses. In the next chapter, ginger, with limes, chilies and herbs adds sparkle to fish and seafood recipes. Then meat and poultry dishes draw on ginger's incredibly varied international heritage. Vegetarian ideas carry on the theme, enlivening grains and vegetables. Lastly comes a luscious array of desserts and cakes, rounding off a mouthwatering exploration of the versatility and deliciousness of this unique spice.

TYPES OF GINGER

FRESH GINGER ROOT

A fresh knobbly root with a smooth, plump appearance and a pale tan colored skin. Any wrinkling  indicates that the ginger is past its best. Once the skin has been peeled away, the ginger is a pale yellowy color and should be firm to the touch, with a fresh, spicy fragrance. The most delicate flesh of the ginger is just below the skin, under this layer it becomes tougher with a slightly woody texture.

DRIED GINGER ROOT

This is very different from the fresh form, and is no substitute for fresh ginger root. The whole root can be used in mixtures of pickling spices and requires bruising to release the flavor.

CRYSTALLIZED GINGER

Ginger is preserved in sugar syrup and then thickly

 coated in crystallized sugar and used as a flavoring in baking, or added to desserts such as ice cream.

GROUND GINGER

The ground form of dried ginger root, it has a hot, spicy flavor and is an essential spice in cakes, gingerbread and ginger cookies. It is also used in savory dishes such as curries and soups, often in combination with other spices.

PRESERVED GINGER

Tender, young shoots of ginger are cooked and preserved in sugar syrup. Both the ginger and the syrup can be used in cakes, sauces and ice cream. The syrup can be added to marinades for savory dishes to give a sweet, gingery flavor.

PICKLED GINGER

Thin slices of ginger are preserved in sweetened vinegar and are used as a garnish for raw fish and served with sushi and other oriental foods. It has a very peppery, pungent flavor, and if added to a dish for its flavor, is removed before serving.

Sliced Ginger Root

Dried Ginger Root

Fresh Ginger Root

Ginger pulp

Pickled ginger

Crystallized ginger

Preserved ginger

Fresh Ginger Root

Ground ginger

$\mathcal{B}$ASIC $\mathcal{T}$ECHNIQUES

—— PREPARING GINGER ROOT ——

Break up the ginger into easily peelable pieces, avoiding very knobbly areas. Using a small sharp knife or vegetable peeler, peel off the skin very thinly and discard. The skin should be smooth and blemish free.

When adding to a recipe during cooking, slice the ginger. After peeling the ginger, cut into thin slices with a sharp knife.

If the ginger root is to be used as a flavoring at the beginning of a recipe, chop finely. When the ginger is to be stir-fried with other ingredients or used as a garnish for finished dishes, cut first into slices, then into fine julienne strips.

GINGER ROOT TIPS

• *Buying fresh ginger root*: choose plump ginger with firm flesh and thin, smooth skin.

• *Storage*: unpeeled ginger root will keep for up to four weeks in the salad drawer of the fridge if wrapped tightly in plastic wrap. Once it begins to wrinkle and take on a dry appearance, discard.

• *Grating*: peel the ginger, then grate finely. Add to sauces, soups, stews and marinades. Chop, grate or slice as required. 1 inch fresh ginger root yields about 1 tablespoon finely chopped ginger root.

• If the ginger sprouts, chop the sprouts and use as a herb, added to salads.

— MAKING GINGER PULP —

Ginger is often used in savory recipes and it can be time-consuming to peel and process it everytime. It's much easier to make the pulp in large quantities and use as needed. To store the pulp, either transfer to an airtight container or jar and refrigerate for four to six weeks, or freeze in ice-cube trays kept specially for the purpose. Add 1 teaspoon of the pulp to each cube space, freeze, then remove from the tray and store in the freezer in a plastic bag. Remove the pulp when needed, and add, while still frozen, to curries or stews.

Peel about 8 ounces fresh ginger root and place in a food processor or blender. Process until pulped, adding a little water to get the right consistency, if necessary.

COOK'S TIPS

• Ground ginger is included in many spice mixtures, the most common is garam masala and it is often added to 5-spice powder, a Chinese seasoning. It also appears in pickling spice mixtures.

• Together with ground black pepper, dried or fresh sage and rosemary, ground ginger makes a tasty poultry seasoning.

• An aromatic tea can be made by adding dried ginger to boiling water.

• Fresh ginger root, together with garlic and onion, is mainly used in stir-fries, oriental, Indian and Arab dishes. It has recently become equally popular in Western countries where it is often added to marinades and used to ginger up fish and poultry dishes.

COOKING WITH GINGER

If the fresh ginger root is to be used in a stir-fry, heat the wok, then add the oil. When the oil is hot, add the chopped or grated ginger and any other ingredients and stir-fry for 30 seconds.

Ginger juice, made from fresh ginger root, is good in marinades, sauces and salad dressings. To make ginger juice, crush finely chopped or grated fresh ginger in a garlic press.

To make a simple curry paste, blend fresh ginger root with garlic, chili and a little water.

QUICK DESSERTS

● Add 1 tablespoon chopped preserved ginger to fresh, cubed melon with a little of the syrup.

● Chop preserved ginger and sprinkle over poached fruit such as peaches, pears or apples.

● Dice a piece of preserved ginger finely, add to soft icing, and use to ice cakes or cookies.

● Add a little finely chopped preserved ginger to whipped cream and serve with fruit, a fruit crisp, or a steamed pudding.

● Chop some crystallized ginger finely and add to cream or cream cheese, and use as a cake filling.

● Stir some finely chopped preserved or crystallized ginger into whipped cream. Use as a sandwich filling for plain meringues.

FLAVORING WITH GINGER

● Ground ginger and crystallized ginger are used in traditional recipes for gingerbread and ginger cookies.

● Preserved ginger in syrup can be used as a flavoring in baking and added to ice cream and other desserts. It is also delicious in cakes, mousses and sauces, and even savory dishes. Stem ginger is specially selected for preservation, being made from the choicest, most tender shoots from the ginger root.

RHUBARB AND GINGER JAM   Makes about 4 pounds

Ginger and rhubarb are the perfect flavor combination in this spicy, tart jam.

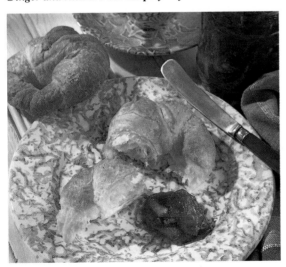

Place 1 tablespoon grated, fresh ginger root and 2¾ pounds trimmed rhubarb into a preserving pan. Add 2½ pounds granulated sugar, the rind and juice of half a lemon, and two peeled, cored and diced, tart apples. Cover the pan and cook over gentle heat until the sugar has melted and the fruits have yielded liquid. When the sugar has completely dissolved, uncover and boil until the temperature reaches the jam setting point on a sugar thermometer, 225°F. Or transfer a small spoonful of jam to a cold saucer, cool a little, then gently push the jam with a finger. If set, it will wrinkle.

Soups and First Courses

Fresh ginger makes an aromatic addition to all sorts

of first courses – it adds a spicy fragrance to even the

simplest soup, and its distinctive flavor is perfect

in oriental-style dishes.

LEEK, PARSNIP AND GINGER SOUP

A flavorful winter warmer, with the added spiciness of fresh ginger.

Serves 4–6

2 tablespoons olive oil

8 ounces leeks, sliced

2 tablespoons finely chopped fresh ginger root

1½ pounds parsnips, roughly chopped

1¼ cups dry white wine, such as Sauvignon blanc

5 cups vegetable broth or water

salt and ground black pepper

low-fat ricotta cheese, to garnish

paprika, to garnish

Heat the oil in a large pan and add the leeks and ginger. Cook gently for 2–3 minutes, until the leeks start to soften. Add the parsnips and cook for a further 7–8 minutes.

Pour in the wine and broth or water and bring to a boil. Reduce the heat and simmer for 20–30 minutes or until the parsnips are tender.

Purée in a food processor or blender until smooth. Season to taste. Reheat and garnish with a swirl of ricotta cheese and a light dusting of paprika.

COOK'S TIP

For an extra gingery flavor, garnish the soup with very finely shredded ginger root.

THAI CHICKEN AND SHRIMP SOUP

Fresh ginger adds a sharp, refreshing tang to this hot and spicy soup.

Serves 4–6

2 × 6-ounce chicken breasts, on
   the bone

1/2 chicken stock cube

1²/₃ cups canned coconut milk

3-inch piece lemon grass

³/₄-inch piece fresh ginger root,
   finely chopped

2 garlic cloves, crushed

2 tablespoons chopped cilantro root,
   or stem

2–3 small red chilies, seeded and
   finely chopped

2 tablespoons fish sauce

5 teaspoons sugar

1/2 teaspoon salt

2 lime leaves

8 ounces fresh or cooked shrimp tails,
   peeled and de-veined

juice of 1 lime

4 cilantro sprigs, chopped, to garnish

2 scallions, green part only, sliced,
   to garnish

4 large red chilies, sliced, to garnish

Place the chicken in a large saucepan and cover with water. Add the half stock cube, and bring to a boil, the reduce the heat and simmer for 45 minutes. Lift the chicken out of the cooking liquid and set the liquid aside. Discard the skin and bones from the chicken and slice the meat into strips. Return the shredded chicken to the cooking liquid, add the coconut milk and simmer gently.

Finely chop the lemon grass and place in a bowl with the ginger, garlic, cilantro and chilies. Mix thoroughly, then add to the cooking liquid with the fish sauce, sugar, salt and lime leaves. Simmer for a further 20 minutes.

Just before serving, add the shrimp and lime juice. Simmer very gently for 5 minutes. Garnish with the cilantro, scallions and chilies.

GINGERY CHINESE CHICKEN WINGS

These are best eaten with fingers as a first course, so make sure you provide plenty of paper napkins.

Serves 4

12 chicken wings

3 garlic cloves, crushed

2 tablespoons grated fresh ginger root

juice of 1 large lemon

3 tablespoons soy sauce

3 tablespoons clear honey

½ teaspoon chili powder

⅔ cup fresh or canned chicken broth

salt and ground black pepper

lemon wedges, to garnish

Remove the tips (pinions) and use to make the broth, if liked. Cut the wings into two joints.

Mix the garlic, ginger, lemon juice, soy sauce, honey and chili powder together and thoroughly coat the chicken wings in the mixture. Season to taste. Cover with plastic wrap and marinate overnight.

Preheat the oven to 425°F. Remove the chicken wings from the marinade and arrange in a single layer in a roasting pan. Bake for 20–25 minutes, basting at least twice with the marinade during cooking until it is used up.

Place the chicken wings on a serving plate. Add the broth to the marinade in the roasting pan, and bring to a boil. Cook to a syrupy consistency and spoon a little over the wings. Serve hot, garnished with lemon wedges.

COOK'S TIP

If you prefer, use chicken breasts or legs instead of chicken wings. Bake until the juices run clear when pierced with a skewer.

SPICY PEANUT AND GINGER BITES

Serve these spicy rice balls with a crisp green salad and a dipping sauce as a starter or snack.

Makes 16

1 garlic clove, crushed

1 tablespoon finely chopped fresh
  ginger root

¼ teaspoon turmeric

1 teaspoon sugar

½ teaspoon salt

1 teaspoon chili sauce

2 teaspoons fish or soy sauce

2 tablespoons chopped fresh cilantro

juice of ½ lime

½ cup long grain rice, cooked

2 ounces unsalted peanuts, chopped

⅔ cup vegetable oil, for deep-frying

Pound together the garlic, ginger, and turmeric using a pestle and mortar. Add the sugar, salt, chili and fish or soy sauce, cilantro, and lime juice.

Add three quarters of the cooked rice and pound until smooth. Stir in the remainder of the rice. Wet your hands and shape into small balls.

Roll the balls in chopped peanuts to coat evenly. Set aside until ready to cook and serve.

Heat the vegetable oil in a deep-frying pan. Prepare a tray lined with paper towels to drain the rice balls. Deep-fry a few at a time until crisp and golden, remove with a slotted spoon then drain on paper towels.

Fish and Seafood

Combined with other fragrant ingredients, such as
lemon grass, lime and cilantro, ginger brightens up
marinades and adds a savory spiciness to sauces
for fish and shellfish.

FISH WITH MANGO AND GINGER DRESSING

The tasty dressing for this salad combines the flavor of rich mango with ginger, hot chili, and lime.

Serves 4

1 large baguette (French bread)

4 redfish, black bream or porgy, each
*   weighing about 10 ounces*

1 tablespoon vegetable oil

1 mango

1 tablespoon grated fresh ginger root

1 fresh red chili, seeded and
*   finely chopped*

2 tablespoons lime juice

2 tablespoons chopped fresh cilantro

6 ounces young spinach

6 ounces cherry tomatoes, halved

Preheat the oven to 350°F. Cut the baguette into 8-inch lengths. Slice lengthwise, then cut into thick fingers. Place the bread on a cookie sheet and dry in the oven for 15 minutes. Preheat the broiler or light the barbecue. Slash the fish on both sides and moisten with oil. Broil or barbecue for about 6 minutes, turning once. Slice one half of the mango and reserve.

Place the remainder in a blender or food processor. Add the ginger, chili, lime juice, and cilantro. Process until smooth. Adjust to a pouring consistency with 2–3 tablespoons water.

Wash and dry the spinach, then arrange on four plates. Place the fish on top. Spoon on the dressing. Serve with mango slices, tomatoes and the bread.

COOK'S TIP

Other varieties of fish suitable
for use in this salad include
salmon, monkfish, tuna, sea
bass, and halibut.

BROILED SNAPPER WITH MANGO SALSA

A ripe mango is used in this fruity salsa with the tropical flavors of cilantro, ginger and chili.

Serves 4

12 ounces new potatoes

3 eggs

4 ounces green beans, trimmed
and halved

4 × 12-ounce red snapper, scaled
and gutted

2 tablespoons olive oil

6 ounces mixed lettuce leaves, such as
frisée or oak leaf

2 cherry tomatoes

salt and ground black pepper

For the salsa

3 tablespoons chopped fresh cilantro

1 medium-size ripe mango, peeled,
pitted and diced

1/2 red chili, seeded and chopped

1 tablespoon grated fresh ginger root

juice of 2 limes

generous pinch of celery salt

Bring the potatoes to a boil and simmer for 15–20 minutes. Drain. Bring another large saucepan of salted water to a boil. Put in the eggs and boil for 4 minutes, then add the beans and cook for a further 6 minutes. Remove the eggs from the pan, cool, peel and cut into quarters. Preheat the broiler. Slash the snappers on each side, moisten with oil and cook for 12 minutes, turning once. To make the salsa, place the cilantro in a blender or food processor. Add the remaining ingredients and process smoothly.

Arrange the lettuce leaves on four large plates. Arrange the snapper over the lettuce and season to taste. Halve the potatoes and tomatoes, and add with the beans and eggs to the salad. Serve with the salsa.

SCALLOPS WITH GINGER RELISH

Scallops flavored with spicy star anise are perfectly matched with a sharp and refreshing ginger relish.

Serves 4

8 sea scallops

4 whole star anise

2 tablespoons sweet butter

salt and ground white pepper

fresh chervil sprigs and whole star
   anise, to garnish

For the relish

½ cucumber, peeled

salt, for sprinkling

2-inch piece ginger root, peeled

2 teaspoons superfine sugar

3 tablespoons rice wine vinegar

2 teaspoons ginger juice, strained from
   a jar of preserved ginger

sesame seeds, for sprinkling

To make the relish, halve the cucumber lengthwise and scoop out the seeds with a teaspoon. Cut the cucumber into 1-inch pieces, place in a colander and sprinkle with salt. Set aside for 30 minutes. To prepare the scallops, cut each into two or three slices. Coarsely grind the star anise in a pestle and mortar. Place the scallop slices with their roe in a bowl and marinate with the star anise and seasoning for about 1 hour.

Rinse the cucumber and dry on paper towels. Cut the ginger into julienne strips and mix with the remaining relish ingredients. Cover and chill.

Heat the butter in a wok. Add the scallop slices and stir-fry for 2–3 minutes. Garnish with the chervil and star anise, and serve with the relish, sprinkled with sesame seeds.

SEAFOOD KEBABS WITH GINGER AND LIME

This fragrant marinade will guarantee a mouthwatering aroma from the barbecue, and it is equally delicious with chicken or pork.

Serves 4–6

1¼ pounds shrimp and cubed monkfish
selection of prepared vegetables, such
* as red, green or orange bell peppers,*
* zucchini, button mushrooms, red*
* onion and cherry tomatoes*
bay leaves

For the marinade

3 limes
1 tablespoon green cardamom pods
1 onion, finely chopped
1 tablespoon grated fresh ginger root
1 large garlic clove, skinned
* and crushed*
3 tablespoons olive oil

First make the marinade. Finely grate the rind from one lime and squeeze the juice from all of them. Split the cardamom pods and remove the seeds.  Crush the cardamom seeds in a pestle and mortar or with the back of a heavy-bladed knife.

Place the lime rind and juice, crushed cardamom, onion, ginger root, garlic and olive oil in a small bowl and mix together thoroughly. Pour the marinade over the shrimp and monkfish, stir gently, then cover and leave in a cool place for 2–3 hours.

Thread four skewers alternately with the shrimp, monkfish, vegetables and bay leaves. Cook slowly under a hot broiler or over a barbecue, basting occasionally with the marinade, until the shrimp, fish and vegetables are just cooked through and browned on the outside. Serve at once.

Poultry and Meat

Ginger is delicious with meat dishes. It is especially good
with chicken, but is also excellent with beef, lamb and
pork, adding a fresh flavor and warm spiciness
to a variety of dishes.

THAI CHICKEN AND VEGETABLE STIR-FRY

Ginger and lemon grass add the authentic flavor of Thailand to this tasty stir-fry.

Serves 4

1 piece lemon grass (or the rind
of ¹/₂ lemon)

2 tablespoons sunflower oil

1 tablespoon grated fresh ginger root

1 large garlic clove, chopped

10 ounces lean chicken, thinly sliced

¹/₂ red bell pepper, seeded and sliced

¹/₂ green bell pepper, seeded and sliced

4 scallions, chopped

2 medium carrots, cut into matchsticks

4 ounces fine green beans

2 tablespoons oyster sauce

pinch of sugar

salt and ground black pepper

¹/₄ cup salted peanuts, lightly crushed,
and cilantro leaves, to garnish

COOK'S TIP

Make this quick supper dish a
little hotter by adding more fresh
ginger root, if you wish.

Thinly slice the lemon grass or lemon rind. Heat the oil in a frying pan over a high heat until hazy. Add the lemon grass or lemon rind, ginger and garlic, and stir-fry for 30 seconds until brown.

Add the chicken and stir-fry for 2 minutes. Then add the vegetables and stir-fry for 4–5 minutes, until the chicken is cooked and the vegetables are almost cooked.

Finally stir in the oyster sauce, sugar and seasoning to taste and stir-fry for another minute to mix and blend well. Serve at once, sprinkled with the peanuts and cilantro leaves and accompanied with rice.

CHICKEN WITH GINGER COUSCOUS

Couscous varies from country to country in North Africa. In this version, both the sauce and the grain are fragrantly spiced with cinnamon and ginger.

Serves 4

2 tablespoons sunflower oil

4 chicken pieces

2 onions, finely chopped

2 garlic cloves, crushed

1 tablespoon grated fresh ginger root

1/2 teaspoon ground cinnamon

1/4 teaspoon ground turmeric

2 tablespoons orange juice

2 teaspoons honey

salt and ground black pepper

fresh mint sprigs, to garnish

For the couscous

2 cups couscous

1 teaspoon salt

2 teaspoons sugar

2 tablespoons sunflower oil

1/2 teaspoon ground cinnamon

1/2 teaspoon ground ginger

2 tablespoons golden raisins

1/2 cup chopped blanched almonds

3 tablespoons chopped pistachios

Heat the oil in a large pan and add the chicken pieces, skin side down. Fry for 3–4 minutes, until the skin is golden, then turn over.

Add the onions, garlic, ginger, spices and a pinch of salt and pour over the orange juice and 1¼ cups water. Cover the pan and bring to a boil, then reduce the heat and simmer for about 30 minutes.

Meanwhile, place the couscous and salt in a bowl and cover with 1½ cups water. Stir once and leave the couscous to stand for 5 minutes. Add the sugar, 1 tablespoon of the oil, the cinnamon, ginger and golden raisins to the couscous and mix very well.

Heat the remaining 1 tablespoon of the oil in a pan and lightly fry the almonds until golden. Stir into the couscous with the pistachios.

Line a steamer with parchment paper and spoon in the couscous. Sit the steamer over the chicken (or over a separate pan of boiling water) and steam for 10 minutes.

Remove the steamer and keep covered. Stir the honey into the chicken liquid and boil rapidly for 3–4 minutes. Spoon the couscous on to a warmed serving platter and top with the chicken and a little of the sauce spooned over. Garnish with mint sprigs and serve with the remaining sauce.

STIR-FRIED GINGER CHICKEN

This Southeast Asian-style stir-fry is colorful, quick to make, and full of flavor.

Serves 4

10 ounces Chinese egg noodles

2 tablespoons vegetable oil

3 scallions, chopped

1 garlic clove, crushed

1 tablespoon grated fresh ginger root

1 teaspoon hot paprika

1 teaspoon ground coriander

3 boneless chicken breasts, sliced

*1 cup sugar-snap peas, topped
and tailed*

4 ounces baby corn, halved

1 cup fresh bean sprouts

1 tablespoon cornstarch

3 tablespoons soy sauce

3 tablespoons lemon juice

1 tablespoon sugar

*3 tablespoons chopped fresh cilantro or
scallion tops, to garnish*

Bring a large saucepan of salted water to a boil. Add the noodles and cook according to the package instructions. Drain, cover and keep warm.

Heat the oil in a wok or large frying pan. Add the scallions and cook over a gentle heat for a minute or two. Add the garlic, ginger root, paprika, coriander and mix well, then stir in the chicken. Stir-fry for 3–4 minutes, then add the sugar-snap peas, baby corn and beansprouts and steam briefly. Add the noodles.

Combine the cornstarch, soy sauce, lemon juice and sugar in a small bowl. Add to the wok or frying pan and simmer briefly to thicken, stirring all the time. Serve garnished with chopped cilantro or scallion tops.

CHICKEN BIRYANI

A spiced Indian rice dish, flavored with ginger and delicately scented with saffron, is layered with chicken and tomatoes, and is a favorite for special occasions. It is delicious served with plain yogurt.

Serves 4

1½ cups basmati rice, rinsed

½ teaspoon salt

5 whole green cardamom pods

2–3 whole cloves

1 cinnamon stick

3 tablespoons vegetable oil

3 onions, sliced

1½ pounds boneless, skinless chicken

¼ teaspoon ground cloves

½ teaspoon ground cardamom

¼ teaspoon hot chili powder

1 teaspoon ground cumin

1 teaspoon ground coriander

½ teaspoon ground black pepper

3 garlic cloves, finely chopped

1 tablespoon chopped fresh ginger root

juice of 1 lemon

4 tomatoes, sliced

2 tablespoons chopped fresh cilantro

⅔ cup natural yogurt

½ teaspoon saffron strands

*3 tablespoons toasted flaked almonds
  and fresh cilantro sprigs, to garnish*

Preheat the oven to 375°F. Bring a pan of water to a boil and add the rice, salt, cardamom pods, cloves and cinnamon stick. Boil for 2 minutes and then drain, leaving the whole spices in the rice.

Heat the oil in a pan and fry the onions for about 8 minutes, until browned. Cube the chicken and add to the pan followed by all the ground spices, the garlic, ginger and lemon juice. Stir-fry for 5 minutes.

Transfer the chicken mixture to a casserole and lay the tomatoes on top. Sprinkle over the fresh cilantro, spoon over the yogurt and top with the drained rice. Soak the saffron in 2 teaspoons hot milk, then drizzle the saffron and milk over the rice and pour over ⅔ cup water.

Cover tightly and bake in the oven for 1 hour. Transfer to a warmed serving platter and remove the whole spices from the rice. Garnish with toasted almonds and fresh cilantro. Serve with yogurt, if you like.

CHINESE-STYLE BEEF WITH GINGER

Toasted sesame seeds and fresh ginger add an oriental flavor to this dish.

Serves 4

1 pound rump steak

2 tablespoons sesame seeds

1 tablespoon sesame oil

2 tablespoons vegetable oil

4 ounces small mushrooms, quartered

1 large green bell pepper, seeded and diced

4 scallions, chopped diagonally

For the marinade

2 teaspoons cornstarch

2 tablespoons rice wine or sherry

1 tablespoon lemon juice

1 tablespoon soy sauce

few drops of Tabasco sauce

2 tablespoon grated fresh ginger root

1 garlic clove, crushed

Trim the steak and cut into thin strips about ½ × 2 inches. Place the sesame seeds in a large frying pan or wok. Cook dry, over moderate heat, shaking the pan until the seeds are golden. Set aside.

To make the marinade, blend the cornstarch with the rice wine or sherry in a bowl, then stir in the lemon juice, soy sauce, Tabasco sauce, ginger root and garlic. Add the beef to the marinade, stir thoroughly, then leave to marinate for 1–2 hours in the fridge.

Heat the oils in the frying pan or wok. Drain the beef, reserving the marinade, and brown a few pieces at a time. Remove the beef with a slotted spoon and keep warm. Add the vegetables to the pan and stir-fry for 2–3 minutes. Remove with a slotted spoon and keep warm. Add the reserved marinade to the pan and cook, stirring until thickened. Return the beef and vegetables to the pan and heat through. Serve with rice or noodles.

INDONESIAN PORK AND SHRIMP RICE

Also known as Nasi Goreng, this is an attractive way of using up leftovers and appears in many variations throughout Indonesia. Rice is the main ingredient, and chilies and ginger are added for additional color and flavor.

Serves 4–6

3 eggs

4 tablespoons vegetable oil

6 shallots, or 1 large onion, chopped

2 garlic cloves, crushed

1 tablespoon chopped fresh ginger root

3 small red chilies, seeded and chopped

1 tablespoon fish sauce

½ teaspoon ground turmeric

6 teaspoons unsweetened cream
of coconut

juice of 2 limes

2 teaspoons sugar

¾ pound lean pork, sliced

¾ pound fresh or cooked shrimp tails

¾ cup bean sprouts

¾ cup Napa cabbage, shredded

1 cup frozen peas, thawed

1½ cups long grain rice, cooked

salt

chopped fresh cilantro, to garnish

In a bowl, beat the eggs with a pinch of salt. Heat a nonstick frying pan over a moderate heat. Pour in the eggs and swirl around the pan to give a thin, even layer. Cook until set, roll up tightly, slice thinly, cover and set aside.

Heat 1 tablespoon of the oil in a wok and fry the shallots or onion until evenly brown. Remove from pan, set aside and keep warm.

Heat the remaining 3 tablespoons of oil in the wok, add the garlic, ginger and chilies, and soften without coloring. Stir in the fish sauce, turmeric, cream of coconut, lime juice, sugar, and salt to taste. Combine briefly over a moderate heat. Add the pork and shrimp, and fry for 3–4 minutes.

Toss the bean sprouts, Napa cabbage, and peas in the spices and cook briefly. Add the rice and stir-fry for 6–8 minutes, stirring to prevent it from burning. Transfer to a large serving plate, decorate with shredded omelet, the fried shallots or onion, and chopped fresh cilantro.

BEEF STRIPS WITH ORANGE AND GINGER

Tender strips of beef, tangy ginger and crisp carrot make a simple but delicious stir-fry.

Serves 4

1 pound lean beef rump, fillet,
or sirloin

finely grated rind and juice of 1 orange

1 tablespoon light soy sauce

1 teaspoon cornstarch

1 tablespoon chopped ginger root

2 teaspoons sesame oil

1 large carrot, cut into thin strips

2 scallions, thinly sliced

Cut the beef into thin strips crosswise using a large sharp knife. Place the beef strips in a bowl and sprinkle over the orange rind and juice. Leave to marinate in a cool place for at least 30 minutes, or overnight in the fridge.

When ready to cook, drain the liquid from the meat and set aside, then mix the meat with the soy sauce, cornstarch and ginger.

Heat the oil in a wok or large frying pan over a medium-high heat and add the beef. Stir-fry for 1 minute until the meat is lightly colored, then add the carrot and stir-fry for 2–3 minutes more.

Stir in the scallions and the reserved marinating liquid, then cook, stirring constantly, until boiling and thickened. Serve the stir-fry hot with rice noodles or plain boiled rice.

COOK'S TIP

Large wok lids are cumbersome
and can be difficult to store in a
small kitchen. Instead of using a
lid, place a circle of wax paper
over the food surface to retain
the cooking juices.

GINGER AND FIVE-SPICE LAMB

Long, slow cooking in a rich mixture of spices is the secret of success with this aromatic lamb dish which is perfect for an informal supper party.

Serves 4

2–3 tablespoons oil

3–3¹⁄₂-pound leg of lamb, boned
   and cubed

1 onion, chopped

1 tablespoon grated fresh ginger root

1 garlic clove, crushed

1 teaspoon five-spice powder

2 tablespoons hoi-sin sauce

1 tablespoon light soy sauce

1¹⁄₄ cups crushed tomatoes

1 cup lamb broth

1 red bell pepper, seeded and cubed

1 yellow bell pepper, seeded and cubed

2 tablespoons chopped fresh cilantro

1 tablespoon sesame seeds, toasted

salt and ground black pepper

Preheat the oven to 325°F. Heat 2 tablespoons of the oil in a flameproof casserole and brown the lamb in batches over a high heat. Remove the meat and set aside.

Add the onion, ginger and garlic to the casserole with a little more of the oil, if necessary, and cook for about 5 minutes, until softened.

Return the lamb to the casserole. Stir in the five-spice powder, hoi-sin and soy sauces, crushed tomatoes, broth and seasoning. Bring to a boil, then cover and cook in the oven for 1¹⁄₄ hours.

Remove the casserole from the oven, stir in the bell peppers, then cover and return to the oven for 15 minutes more, or until the lamb is tender.

Sprinkle with the cilantro and sesame seeds. Serve hot.

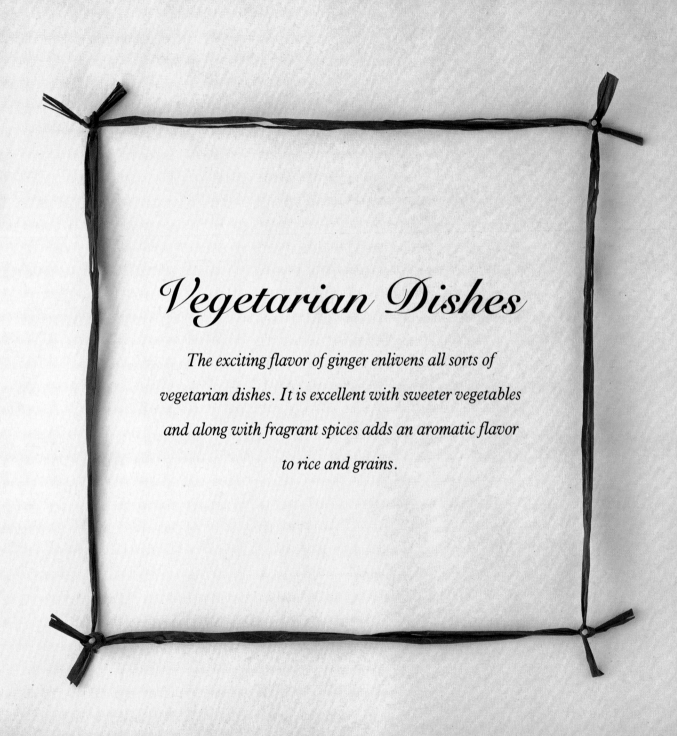

Vegetarian Dishes

The exciting flavor of ginger enlivens all sorts of vegetarian dishes. It is excellent with sweeter vegetables and along with fragrant spices adds an aromatic flavor to rice and grains.

VEGETABLE, CHILI AND GINGER CURRY

A tasty mid-week curry to serve with rice such as brown basmati, small poppadums and cucumber raita.

Serves 4

2 garlic cloves, chopped

1 tablespoon chopped fresh ginger root

1 fresh green chili, seeded and chopped

1 tablespoon oil

1 onion, sliced

1 large potato, chopped

2 tablespoons ghee or softened butter

1 tablespoon curry powder, mild or hot

1 medium-size cauliflower, cut into
   small florets

2½ cups broth

2 tablespoons unsweetened cream
   of coconut

salt and ground black pepper

10 ounce can fava beans, with liquor

juice of half a lemon (optional)

chopped fresh cilantro or parsley,
   to serve

Blend the garlic, ginger, chili and oil in a blender or food processor until a smooth paste is formed.

In a large saucepan, fry the onion and potato in the ghee or butter for 5 minutes then stir in the spice paste and curry powder. Cook for 1 minute.

Add the cauliflower florets and stir well into the spicy mixture, then pour in the broth. Bring to a boil and mix in the coconut, stirring until it melts.

Season well, then cover and simmer for 10 minutes. Add the beans and their liquor and cook uncovered for a further 10 minutes.

Check the seasoning and add a good squeeze of lemon juice if liked. Serve hot garnished with fresh cilantro or parsley.

HERB CREPES WITH TOMATO AND GINGER SAUCE

These mouth-watering light herb crêpes with ginger-flavored sauce make a delicious starter, or serve with a crisp salad for a light lunch. Use a mixture of herbs such as parsley, thyme and chervil.

Serves 4

2 tablespoons chopped fresh herbs
a little sunflower oil
½ cup milk
3 eggs
¼ cup flour
pinch of salt

For the sauce

2 tablespoons olive oil
1 small onion, chopped
2 garlic cloves, crushed
1 tablespoon grated fresh ginger root
14-ounce can chopped tomatoes

For the filling

1 pound fresh spinach
¾ cup ricotta cheese
2 tablespoons pine nuts, toasted
5 sun-dried tomatoes, chopped
2 tablespoons shredded fresh basil
salt, nutmeg and ground black pepper
4 egg whites

To make the crêpes, place the herbs and 1 tablespoon oil in a blender or food processor and blend until smooth. Add the milk, eggs, flour and salt and blend again until smooth. Let stand for 30 minutes. Heat a small nonstick crêpe or frying pan and add a very small amount of oil. Pour out any excess oil and pour in a ladleful of the batter. Swirl to cover the base. Cook for 1–2 minutes, turn and cook the other side. Repeat with the remaining batter to make 8 crêpes.

To make the sauce, heat the oil in a small pan. Add the onion, garlic and ginger and cook gently for 5 minutes until softened. Add the tomatoes and cook for a further 10–15 minutes until thickened. Purée in a blender or food processor, strain and set aside. To make the filling, wash the spinach, removing any large stalks, and place in a large pan with only the water that clings to the leaves. Cover and cook until the spinach has just wilted. Remove from the heat and refresh in cold water. Place in a strainer, squeeze out the excess water and chop finely. Mix the spinach with the ricotta, pine nuts, sun-dried tomatoes and basil. Season with salt, nutmeg and pepper.

Preheat the oven to 375°F. Whisk the 4 egg whites until they form stiff peaks but are not dry. Fold one-third into the spinach and ricotta to lighten the mixture, then gently fold in the rest. Place a large spoonful of filling on each crêpe and fold into quarters. Place on an oiled cookie sheet. Repeat until all the filling and crêpes are used up. Bake in the oven for 10–15 minutes or until set. Reheat the tomato sauce to serve with the crêpes.

MUSHROOM AND OKRA CURRY WITH GINGERY MANGO RELISH

This simple but delicious curry with its fresh gingery mango relish is best served with plain basmati rice.

Serves 4

4 garlic cloves, chopped

1 tablespoon chopped ginger root

1–2 red chilies, seeded and chopped

¾ cup cold water

1 tablespoon sunflower oil

1 teaspoon coriander seeds

1 teaspoon cumin seeds

1 teaspoon ground cumin

½ teaspoon ground cardamom

pinch of ground turmeric

14-ounce can chopped tomatoes

1 pound mushrooms, halved

8 ounces okra, trimmed and cut into
   ½-inch slices

2 tablespoons chopped fresh cilantro

For the mango relish

1 large ripe mango

1 small garlic clove, crushed

1 onion, finely chopped

2 teaspoons grated fresh ginger root

1 fresh red chili, seeded and chopped

pinch of salt and sugar

For the mango relish, peel the mango and cut off the flesh from the pit. In a bowl mash the mango flesh with a fork or use a blender or food processor, and mix in the rest of the relish ingredients. Set aside.

Place the garlic, ginger, chilies and 3 tablespoons of the water into a blender or food processor and blend until smooth.

Heat the sunflower oil in a large pan. Add the whole coriander and cumin seeds and allow them to sizzle for a few seconds. Add the ground cumin, ground cardamom and turmeric and cook for 1 minute more.

Add the paste from the blender, the tomatoes, remaining water, mushrooms and okra. Stir to mix well and bring to a boil. Reduce the heat, cover, and simmer for 5 minutes.

Remove the cover, turn up the heat slightly and cook for 5–10 minutes more until the okra is tender. Stir in the fresh cilantro and serve with rice and the mango relish.

THAI FRAGRANT RICE WITH GINGER

A lovely, soft, fluffy rice dish, perfumed with fresh ginger and lemon grass.

Serves 4

1 piece of lemon grass

2 limes

1 cup brown basmati rice

1 tablespoon olive oil

1 onion, chopped

1 tablespoon chopped fresh ginger root

1½ teaspoons coriander seeds

1½ teaspoons cumin seeds

3 cups vegetable broth

4 tablespoons chopped fresh cilantro

lime wedges, to serve

Finely chop the lemon grass. Remove the rind from the limes using a zester or fine grater. Rinse the rice in plenty of cold water until the water runs clear. Drain through a strainer.

Heat the oil in a large pan and add the onion, ginger, spices, lemon grass and lime rind and cook gently for 2–3 minutes. Add the rice and cook for another minute, then add the broth and bring to a boil. Reduce the heat and cover the pan. Cook gently for 30 minutes then check the rice. If it is still crunchy, cover the pan again and leave for a further 3–5 minutes. Remove from the heat. Stir in the fresh cilantro, fluff up the grains, cover and leave for 10 minutes. Serve with lime wedges.

COOK'S TIP

Other varieties of rice, such as white basmati or long grain, can be used for this dish but you will need to adjust the cooking times according to the type used.

SPICY GINGER DHAL

If you thought yellow split peas were only for soups, then try this Indian-inspired dish. Serve with rice, chapatis or naan bread and whatever main dish you like.

Serves 4–6

8 ounces yellow split peas

2 onions, chopped

1 large bay leaf

2½ cups broth or water

2 teaspoons black mustard seeds

2 tablespoons butter, melted

1 garlic clove, crushed

1 tablespoon grated fresh ginger root

1 small green bell pepper, sliced

1 teaspoon ground turmeric

1 teaspoon garam masala or mild
  curry powder

3 tomatoes, skinned and chopped

salt and ground black pepper

fresh cilantro or parsley, to serve

Put the split peas, 1 onion and the bay leaf in the broth or water, in a covered pan. Simmer for 25 minutes, seasoning lightly towards the end.

In a separate pan, fry the mustard seeds in the butter for about 30 seconds until they start to pop, then add all the remaining onion, along with the garlic, ginger and green bell pepper.

Sauté for about 5 minutes until softened, then stir in the remaining spices and fry for a few seconds more.

Add the split peas, tomatoes, and a little extra water if needed. Cover and simmer for a further 10 minutes, then check the seasoning and serve hot garnished with cilantro or parsley.

GINGERY VEGETABLE COUSCOUS

This tasty combination of sweet vegetables and spices makes a hearty main dish.

Serves 4

1 generous pinch of saffron threads

1 tablespoon olive oil

1 red onion, sliced

2 garlic cloves, crushed

1–2 fresh red chilies, seeded and
  finely chopped

1-inch piece fresh ginger root, chopped

½ teaspoon ground cinnamon

14-ounce can chopped tomatoes

1¼ cups vegetable broth

4 carrots, sliced

2 turnips, cubed

1 pound sweet potatoes, cubed

⅓ cup raisins

2 zucchini, sliced

14-ounce can chick-peas, drained
  and rinsed

3 tablespoons chopped fresh parsley

3 tablespoons chopped fresh cilantro

1 pound quick-cook couscous

Let the saffron infuse in a small bowl in 3 tablespoons boiling water for about 30 minutes. Heat the oil in a large saucepan. Add the onion, garlic and chilies and cook gently for 5 minutes.

Add the chopped ginger and cinnamon and cook for a further 1–2 minutes until softened.

Add the tomatoes, broth, infused saffron and liquid, carrots, turnips, sweet potatoes and raisins, cover and simmer for 25 minutes.

Add the zucchini, chick-peas, parsley and cilantro and cook for 10 minutes more until all the vegetables are cooked.

Meanwhile prepare the couscous following the package instructions and serve with the vegetables.

LEMON AND GINGER SPICY BEANS

An extremely quick delicious meal, made with canned beans for speed.

Serves 4

2 tablespoons chopped fresh ginger root

3 garlic cloves, roughly chopped

1 cup cold water

1 tablespoon sunflower oil

1 large onion, thinly sliced

1 fresh red chili, seeded and
  finely chopped

1/4 teaspoon cayenne pepper

2 teaspoons ground cumin

1 teaspoon ground coriander

1/2 teaspoon ground turmeric

2 tablespoons lemon juice

1/2 cup chopped fresh cilantro

14-ounce can black-eyed peas, drained
  and rinsed

14-ounce can aduki beans, drained
  and rinsed

14-ounce can navy beans, drained
  and rinsed

salt and ground black pepper

Place the ginger, garlic and 4 tablespoons of the cold water in a blender or food processor and blend until smooth. Set aside.

Heat the oil in a pan. Add the onion and chili and cook gently for 5 minutes until the vegetables are softened.

Add the cayenne pepper, cumin, ground coriander and turmeric and stir-fry for 1 minute.

Stir in the ginger and garlic paste from the blender and cook for another minute, stirring to prevent sticking.

Add the remaining water, lemon juice and fresh cilantro, stir well and bring to a boil. Cover the pan tightly and cook for 5 minutes.

Add all the beans and cook for a further 5–10 minutes. Season with salt and pepper to taste and serve.

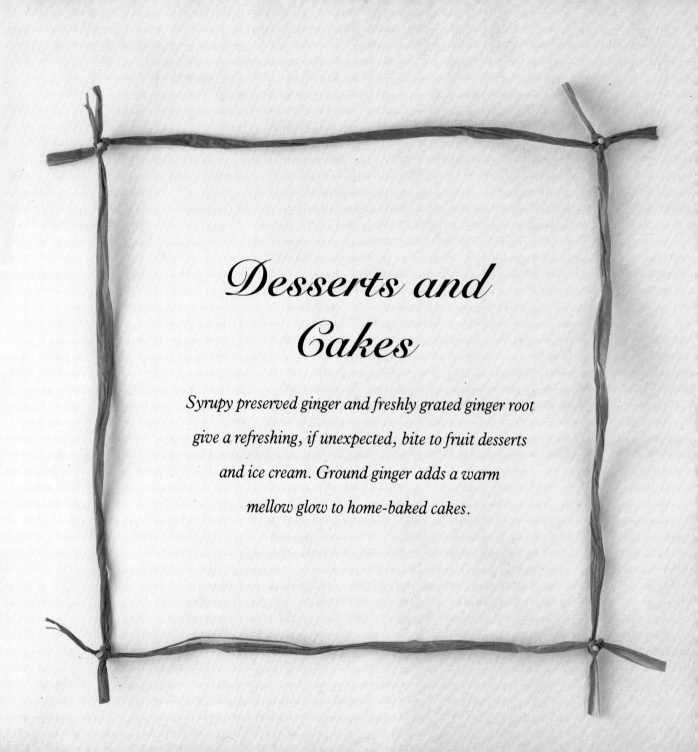

Desserts and Cakes

Syrupy preserved ginger and freshly grated ginger root

give a refreshing, if unexpected, bite to fruit desserts

and ice cream. Ground ginger adds a warm

mellow glow to home-baked cakes.

GOLDEN GINGER COMPOTE

Warm, spicy and full of sun-ripened ingredients – this is the perfect winter dessert.

Serves 4

2 cups kumquats

1 1/4 cups dried apricots

2 tablespoons golden raisins

1 2/3 cups water

1 orange

1 tablespoon grated fresh ginger root

4 green cardamom pods

4 cloves

2 tablespoons clear honey

1 tablespoon sliced almonds, toasted

Wash the kumquats, and, if they are large, cut them in half. Place them in a pan with the apricots, golden raisins and water. Bring to a boil.

Pare the rind thinly from the orange and add to the pan. Add the ginger to the pan. Lightly crush the green cardamom pods and add them to the pan, along with the cloves.

Reduce the heat, cover the pan and let simmer gently for about 30 minutes, or until the fruit is tender, stirring occasionally.

Squeeze the juice from the orange and add to the pan with honey to taste, sprinkle with sliced almonds and serve warm.

COOK'S TIP

Use ready-to-eat dried apricots.
Reduce the liquid to about 1 1/4
cups, and add the apricots for
the last 5 minutes of cooking.

55

MANGO AND GINGER CLOUDS

The sweet, perfumed flavor of ripe mango combines beautifully with ginger, and this low-fat dessert makes the very most of them both.

Serves 6

3 ripe mangoes

3 pieces preserved ginger in syrup

3 tablespoons preserved ginger syrup

½ cup silken tofu

3 egg whites

6 pistachios, chopped

Cut the mangoes in half and remove the pits. Peel and coarsely chop the flesh. Put the mango flesh in a blender or food processor, with the preserved ginger, ginger syrup and tofu. Blend the mixture until smooth, then spoon into a bowl. Put the egg whites in a bowl and whisk them until they form soft peaks. Fold them lightly into the mango mixture. Spoon the mixture into wide dishes or glasses and chill before serving, sprinkled with the chopped pistachios.

VARIATION

If you prefer, you can serve this dessert lightly frozen. Add the nuts just before serving.

COOK'S TIP

Don't serve raw egg whites to pregnant women, babies, young children, the elderly, or anyone who is ill.

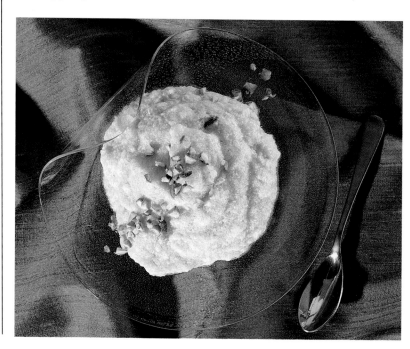

WATERMELON, GINGER AND GRAPEFRUIT SALAD

This combination of fruit and ginger is very light and refreshing for a summer meal.

Serves 4

2 cups diced watermelon flesh

2 ruby or pink grapefruit

2 pieces preserved ginger in syrup

2 tablespoons preserved ginger syrup

COOK'S TIP

Toss the fruits gently –
grapefruit segments will break
up easily and the appearance of
the dish will be spoiled.

Remove any seeds from the watermelon and cut the flesh into bite-size chunks. Using a small sharp knife, cut away all the peel and pith from the grapefruits and carefully lift out the segments, catching any juice.

Finely chop the preserved ginger and place in a serving bowl with the melon cubes and grapefruit segments, adding the reserved juice. Spoon the ginger syrup over the fruits and toss lightly together.

GINGERBREAD UPSIDE-DOWN CAKE

This rich, gingery dessert is quite quick to make and looks very impressive.

Serves 4–6

sunflower oil, for brushing

1 tablespoon brown sugar

4 medium peaches, halved and pitted,
  or canned peach halves

8 walnut halves

For the base

1 cup whole-wheat flour

1/2 teaspoon baking soda

1 1/2 teaspoons ground ginger

1 teaspoon ground cinnamon

1/2 cup brown sugar

1 egg

1/2 cup skim milk

1/4 cup sunflower oil

Preheat the oven to 350°F. For the topping, brush the base and sides of a 9-inch round springform pan with oil. Sprinkle the sugar over the base. Arrange the peaches cut-side down in the pan with a walnut half in each.

For the base, sift together the flour, baking soda, ginger, and cinnamon, then stir in the sugar. Beat together the egg, milk and oil, then mix into the dry ingredients until smooth.

Pour the mixture evenly over the peaches and bake in the preheated oven for 35–40 minutes, until firm to the touch. Turn out on to a serving plate. Serve hot with yogurt or ice cream.

GINGER ICE CREAM

Preserved ginger adds a delicious spiciness to this creamy, refreshing ice cream.

Serves 4–6

2 cups milk

4-inch vanilla bean

4 egg yolks

6 tablespoons granulated sugar

4 pieces preserved ginger, chopped

2 tablespoons preserved ginger syrup

Make the custard sauce. Heat the milk with the vanilla bean in a saucepan without letting it boil. Remove from the heat. Beat the egg yolks and gradually add the sugar. Beat for about 5 minutes. Add the milk gradually through a strainer, stirring constantly. Discard the vanilla bean. Pour the mixture into the top of a double boiler, and add the ginger. Stir over moderate heat until the custard sauce thickens enough to coat the back of a spoon. Add the ginger syrup. Remove from the heat and let cool.

Freeze in an ice-cream maker, or freeze, process, and freeze again.

BANANA GINGER CAKE

This ginger cake is moist and sticky. It keeps well and improves with keeping. Store it in a covered container for up to two months.

Makes 1 cake

1¾ cups flour

2 teaspoons baking soda

2 teaspoons ground ginger

1¾ cups oatmeal

4 tablespoons brown sugar

6 tablespoons sunflower margarine

⅔ cup corn syrup

1 egg, beaten

3 ripe bananas, mashed

¾ cup confectioner's sugar

preserved ginger, to decorate (optional)

Preheat the oven to 325°F. Grease and line a 7- × 11-inch cake pan. Sift together the flour, baking soda and ginger into a large bowl, then stir in the oatmeal.

Melt the sugar, margarine and syrup in a saucepan over low heat, then leave to cool for a few minutes before stirring into the flour mixture. Beat in the egg and mashed bananas.

Spoon into the pan and bake for about 1 hour, or until firm to the touch. Allow to cool in the pan, then turn out and cut into squares.

Sift the confectioner's sugar into a bowl and stir in just enough water to make a smooth, runny icing. Drizzle the icing over each square and top with a piece of preserved ginger, if you like.

COOK'S TIP

This is a nutritious, energy-giving cake that is a really good choice for packed lunches as it doesn't break up too easily.

PINEAPPLE AND GINGER CAKE

This tasty cake is packed with flavors; apricot and pineapple are combined with tangy orange and lemon, and spiked with the refreshing, peppery taste of ginger.

Serves 10–12

¾ cup sweet butter

¾ cup superfine sugar

3 eggs, beaten

few drops of vanilla extract

2 cups flour, sifted

¼ teaspoon salt

1½ teaspoons baking powder

1⅓ cups ready-to-eat dried apricots, chopped

½ cup each chopped crystallized ginger and crystallized pineapple

grated rind and juice of ½ orange

grated rind and juice of ½ lemon

a little milk

Preheat the oven to 350°F. Double line an 8-inch round or 7-inch square cake pan. Cream the butter and sugar together until light and fluffy.

Gradually beat the eggs into the creamed mixture with the vanilla extract, beating well after each addition. Sift together the flour, salt and baking powder into a bowl, and add a little to the mixture with the last of the egg, then fold in the rest.

Fold in the fruit, ginger and fruit rinds gently, then add sufficient fruit juice and milk to give a fairly soft dropping consistency.

Spoon the mixture into the prepared pan and smooth the top with a wet spoon. Bake for 20 minutes, then reduce the oven temperature to 325°F for a further 1½–2 hours, or until firm to the touch and a skewer comes out of the center clean.

Leave the cake to cool in the pan completely, then turn out and wrap in fresh paper before storing in an airtight tin.

COOK'S TIP
This is not a long-keeping cake, but it does freeze, well-wrapped in waxed paper and then overwrapped in foil.

INDEX